Samuel Bowles

The Pacific Railroad

How to Go and What to See

Samuel Bowles

The Pacific Railroad
How to Go and What to See

ISBN/EAN: 9783744649421

Printed in Europe, USA, Canada, Australia, Japan

Cover: Foto ©Andreas Hilbeck / pixelio.de

More available books at **www.hansebooks.com**

THE

PACIFIC RAILROAD—OPEN.

HOW TO GO: WHAT TO SEE.

GUIDE FOR TRAVEL TO AND THROUGH WESTERN AMERICA.

BY

SAMUEL BOWLES,

AUTHOR OF "ACROSS THE CONTINENT," AND "COLORADO, ITS PARKS AND MOUNTAINS."

BOSTON:
FIELDS, OSGOOD, & CO.,
SUCCESSORS TO TICKNOR AND FIELDS.
1869.

Entered according to Act of Congress, in the year 1869, by
FIELDS, OSGOOD, & CO.,
in the Clerk's Office of the District Court of the District of Massachusetts.

UNIVERSITY PRESS: WELCH, BIGELOW, & CO.,
CAMBRIDGE.

CONTENTS.

		PAGE
I.	INTRODUCTORY. — THE GRAND RIDE	5
II.	FROM CHICAGO TO THE ROCKY MOUNTAINS	16
III.	COLORADO	27
IV.	THE MOUNTAINS AND THE MORMONS	43
V.	FROM SALT LAKE TO THE PACIFIC	54
VI.	SAN FRANCISCO	65
VII.	CALIFORNIA AT LARGE	78
VIII.	THE SANDWICH ISLANDS	91
IX.	OREGON. — PUGET'S SOUND. — THE COLUMBIA RIVER	100
X.	IDAHO. — SHOSHONE FALLS	106
XI.	MONTANA AND HOME	110

APPENDIX.

OUTLINES FOR A TWO MONTHS' JOURNEY TO THE PACIFIC STATES BY THE PACIFIC RAILROAD 119

TABLE OF RAILROAD DISTANCES BETWEEN THE ATLANTIC AND PACIFIC OCEANS 121

THE PACIFIC RAILROAD — OPEN.

HOW TO GO: WHAT TO SEE.

I.

INTRODUCTORY. — THE GRAND RIDE.

THE Pacific Railroad — open, is a great fact to America, to the world. The vast regions that it brings, for the first time, into our familiar knowledge hold a new world of nature and of wealth, and are full of delightful surprises for the lover of scenery, the student in science, the seeker of opportunity for power and for riches. It is the unrolling of a new map, the revelation of a new empire, the creation of a new civilization, the revolution of the world's haunts of pleasure and the world's homes of wealth. Europe long ago became only a familiar panorama, with the surprises and sentimentalisms all written in at the proper places, like the "cheers" and "laughter" of a faithfully reported speech. But thanks to the toughness of day and night stage travel for a continuous three weeks; thanks to the greed for gold and the high prices of food, leaving no time for those who had gone into this wide, new land to look at its scenery, or to study its phenomena, or at least to write about them; thanks, indeed, to the Indians, of whom all sentimental travellers have a holy horror; thanks, finally, to the rapidity with which the railroad has been built, we have here a world of nature, fresh and tempting, for the explorer. The field is too broad, also the variety of experiences to be had too great, the forms and freaks of nature too strange and too numerous, — the whole revelation too unique and too astonishing, — to be readily catalogued and put into flexible covers for one's overcoat pocket. So the pleasure of original discovery — delicious victual for our vanity — may not unfairly be enjoyed by those who travel within the next year or two by the Pacific Railroad, and are wise enough, and have leisure enough, to deploy liberally to the right and left, at salient points, along its track.

Near two thirds of all the land of the United States lies beyond the Mississippi, not counting in the outlying purchase of Alaska, which will doubtless prove a very good thing when we have found out what to do with it. The Pacific Railroad fairly bisects this vast area east and west, as the Rocky Mountains — the backbone and dividing line of the continent — do north and south; the two cutting it up into huge quarters, each of which would overlay all Europe this side of Russia, and flap lustily in the wind all around the edges. It will take us long to learn what there is on and in it; how long, indeed, to subjugate it to use and the ministries of civilization! But with one railroad of two thousand miles built across it in four years, and two others to follow within the present generation, our strides in its conquest are at least on equal scale with its majesty and its mysteries.

Skipping the Mississippi valley as more or less

familiar country to us all, and taking up the New West on the other side of the Missouri, where the Pacific Railroad proper begins, there are four great natural divisions in the country hence to the Pacific. First the Plains, that grandest of all glacial deposits, according to Agassiz, five hundred miles wide and one thousand miles long, stretching from river to mountains, from Britain to Mexico; a magnificent earth ocean, rolling up in beautiful green billows along the shores of the continental streams and continental mountains that border it, but calming down in the vast centre as if the Divine voice had here again uttered its "Peace, be still." The ocean does not give deeper sense of illimitable space; never such feeling of endless repose as inspires the traveller amid this unchanging boundlessness. We used to call it The Great American Desert; it is really the great natural pasture-ground of the nation; and the Platte will yet prove the northern Nile. The antelope, the buffalo, and the wolf are already disappearing before the horse, the ox, and the sheep, and these, for so far as the waters of the Platte may be spread, — and volume and fall offer wide promise for that, — will give way in time to fields of corn and wheat.

Next the Mountains, — five hundred miles width of mountains, staying the continent at its centre, and feeding the great waters that fertilize two thirds its area, and keep the two oceans alive. The Cordilleras of South America, the Rocky Mountains of North America, are here broken up into a dozen sub-ranges, with vast elevated plains lying among and between; their crests broken down and wasted away for a pathway for the iron track across the continent. This section is full of natural wonder and beauty, of scientific variety and marvel; in its centre, holding the divide of the continent, lies a great barren basin, without living streams, and almost without living springs, — a desert, indeed, which the trains should always manage to pass over in the night; and beyond, the picturesque descent into Salt Lake valley, past majestic ruins of majestic mountains, under towering walls of granite, along banks of snow and beds of flowers, through narrow canyons with frowning sides, down streams whose waters lead the locomotive a losing race, and turn the train from one novelty to another, from one wonder to a greater, — altogether, perhaps, the most interesting and exciting portion of the whole continental ride.

Now a third stretch of five hundred miles through Utah and Nevada, whose united territory takes in little more than the vast interior basin, which, more properly than any other region in our extended territory, merits the name of the American Desert. The Colorado and its tributaries drain much of its eastern and all its southeastern portions; and some of the shorter branches of the Snake or Columbia cross its northern border; but, with these exceptions, all the waters within its six hundred by three hundred miles' area rise and flow and waste within itself. They contribute nothing to the common stock of the ocean. Salt

Lake is its chief sheet of water, — fifty by one hundred miles in extent, — and is bountifully fed from the western slopes of the Rocky Mountain ranges, but has no visible outlet. The Humboldt River, lying east and west along its upper line, and marking the track of the railroad for some three hundred miles, though fed from various ranges of mountains, that cut the basin every dozen or twenty miles north and south, yet finally weakens and wastes itself in a huge sink within a hundred miles of the California line. So with the fresh streams that pour down on the western border from the Sierra Nevadas, and those of feebler flow from the winter snows of the interior mountain ranges, — all, so soon as they reach the valleys, begin to be rapidly absorbed by the dry air and the drier elements of the soil, and, sooner or later, absolutely die away. Yet, where and while they do exist, there are strips of fertile land that yield most abundantly of grass and grain and vegetables; and where, as in the Salt

Lake valley on the east, and in the Carson on the west, the mountain streams can be divided and spread about in fertilizing ditches, agriculture wins its greatest triumphs.

As a whole, this is a barren and uninteresting country for the general traveller; sodas and salts and sulphurs taint the waters and the soils; the dust, wherever roused, is as searching and poisonous as it is delicate and impalpable; the rare grass is not green, but a sickly yellow or a faint gray; trees and shrubs huddle like starved and frightened sheep into little nooks among the hills, stunted and peevish in growth and character, with no birthright there, and often none visible within the horizon's stretch of ten to twenty miles; no flower dreams of life in such uncongeniality; wastes of volcanic rocks lie along and around rivers that might otherwise be tempted to bless the country they pass through; beds of furious torrents slash the hillsides and mar the valleys; while fields of alkali look in the distance like fresh and refreshing banks of snow, and taunt approach with the suffocating reality. Some of the valleys seem indeed to realize the character of the fabled Death's Valley of southern Nevada, within which no vegetable life ever creeps, out of which no human life ever goes; and yet, within this grand area of distance and desert, two States have risen and are prosperous, — one planted by the fanaticism of a religion, and the other by the fanaticism for gold and silver. To these are we indebted for our path across the continent; while the traveller finds refreshment for his finer senses in the subtle beauty of the air, and the palpitating roundness of the hills that, with the winds for architect, present such forms, unbroken by rock or trees, as are a constant exhilaration to the eye.

The final division of the journey begins with the eastern foot-hills of the Sierra Nevada mountains, and carries us over these, through twice welcome forests, of unaccustomed height and variety; by broad lakes of rare purity and beauty; along rocky precipices, unscaled until the engineer for the railroad planted his level on the walls, and the Chinaman followed with his subduing pick; down by fathomless gorges; through long-delaying foot-hills, waste with the miner's ruthless touch, or green with the vineyards that promise to heal the wounds of nature; out by the muddy Sacramento and its broad alluvials, golden brown with the summer's decay, over long stretches of the tule marshes; under the shadows of Mount Diablo; finally, across the wide inland bay to the sand-hills that the Pacific has thrown up as a barrier to her own restless ambition, and over which San Francisco roughly but rapidly creeps into her position as the second great city of America.

This is but a two hundred miles' ride, and should be made from sun to sun, for it takes the traveller through already fabled lands in our history, and introduces him to that region of wonderful wealth, of contradictory and comprehensive nature, of strange scientific revelations, of fascinations unequalled, of repulsions undisputed, — California, the seat of a new empire, the promised creator of a new race. And here, the traveller's experiences have but just begun; his curiosity is brought only to its edge. Let us go back and look around, and see where he should linger, on what it should feed itself.

II.

FROM CHICAGO TO THE ROCKY MOUNTAINS.

HUMBOLDT, in one of his solemn sentences, prescribes three requisites for travel in new regions : 1, serenity of mind ; 2, passionate love for some class of scientific labor ; 3, a pure feeling for the enjoyment which Nature, in her freedom, is ready to impart. These are all very desirable, at least one is indispensable ; but my companions may swap off the other two for a well-filled purse and a good set of flannels. We may be as serene and scientific and sentimental as the old German traveller himself ; but without these other possessions, we cannot go far or be very comfortable.

Then we must be liberal as to time too ; the average American can see Europe in thirty days, I know ; but this is a bigger job. True, with that limit, he can be carried from Boston to San Francisco in ten days, — allowing for a night or two in bed, and one or two failures to connect at that, — and back in the same time, and have a third ten days to look about him in the mountains, in Utah, and in "Frisco"; and this is better than nothing, of course; but still, comparing what he thinks he knows with what he really does, before and after such a trip, he will be immensely more ignorant when he returns than he was at starting. I cannot tolerate the idea of less than sixty days; and we shall find three months devoted to the journey the busiest and best spent in our lives. That is as little time as any one proposing really to see our interior and Pacific States should allow himself to take for the purpose. So make a ninety-day note for our expenses, — well, say four hundred dollars a month, — the average American traveller, in these greenback days, will hardly get off with less, — and leave a good indorser for any little contingency of delay, such as a pressing invitation to visit a "friendly" Indian village, or a long call from those persuasive gentlemen of the interior basin, "the road agents." We may as well count railroad travel at an average of five cents a mile, and stage at twenty cents, and board and lodging, whether with Pullman or at the hotels, at five dollars a day. Extras and contingencies will need all these allowances have to spare, — if they have any.

Prejudices against sleeping-cars must be conquered at the start. They are a necessity of our long American travel. There are often no inviting or even tolerable places for stopping over night, and, besides, we cannot afford to lose the time, when so much of beauty and interest lies beyond. But the Pullman saloon, sleeping, and restaurant cars of the West — as yet unknown in the Atlantic States — make a different thing of railroad travelling from what it is in the close, cramped, ill-ventilated, dirty box-cars of common experience. They introduce a comfort, even a luxury, into life on the rail that European travel has not yet attained to. For the Pacific Railroad excursions these cars will be offered to private parties on special charter; that is, one or two dozen people may club together, and hire one for their home by day and night as they ride through to the Pacific coast, and back, stopping over with them wherever they choose on the route. By day they are open, roomy, broad-seated cars; by night they offer equally comfortable beds, with clean linen and thick blankets; with as good toilet accommodations as space will allow, and a servant at command constantly. Those with a kitchen furnish a meal to order, equal to that of a first-class restaurant, and with neat and fresh table appointments. But the eating-stations on the whole route already average respectably; some of them are most excellent; and all will soon be at least good. The modern American mind, especially that of the Western type, gives intelligent thought to the food question; and one of the surprises before us is the excellent victuals they will give us on the Pacific coast.

The Pullman cars go along with all through trains, and the independent traveller can make such use of them, day or night, as he chooses to pay for. Those for sleeping only are attached to the trains as night approaches, and dropped in the morning, while the traveller resumes his place in the regular cars of the road. But travellers who can afford the extra expense will choose either to share in a special charter of one for the round trip, or engage a particular seat and berth in a regular one for so far as they may be going without stopping. To understand the advantages of these cars, and learn how best to make use of them, is a part of the education of the traveller in new America. Their introduction and development and popular use mark an era in the history of railroad travel, and place America at the head of nations in its convenience and comfort.

Though Pullman promises to back one of these cars to order up at our very doors in Boston or New York, we shall naturally take up our grand journey at Chicago. This is just one third the way across the continent, and the beginning of the New West, whose spirit is nowhere so proudly rampant, into whose growth no other city so intimately enters. The pulse of the Pacific beats with electric sympathy on the southern shore of Lake Michigan; and if Chicago does not hear every blow of the pick in the depths of the gold-mines of Colorado and Montana, she at least has made sure to furnish the pick, and to have a claim on the gold it brings to light.

One this spring, two this summer, three in the fall, and another year four roads invite us across Illinois and Iowa to the junction of the Pacific road proper on the Missouri River. This five hundred mile ride is through the best of the rich prairie country of the Mississippi Valley. If it is stranger to us, it will arouse our enthusiasm by its wide-reaching openness, the evidences of its fertility, and the signs of its civilization and prosperity; if we have been introduced before, we shall even the more wonder at the rapidity of its growth and the wealth of its accumulating harvests. It is quite worth while to stop a day either on the Mississippi River at Clinton, or Davenport, or Burlington, or at some such town as Geneva or Dixon in Illinois, or Grinnell or Des Moines in Iowa, and see more closely than the cars permit the character and culture of this most interesting region and its population. Last year, before the Pacific Railroad was open, it was the New West; now it is the Old; but it will always be the garden and granary of the continent. It is our new New England; here the Yankee has broadened and softened; and what he can do, what he has done here, with a richer soil, a broader area, a larger hope, and a surer realization, is worth the scrutiny of every American and every student of America. Those who would understand the sources of American wealth, and the courses of American politics and religion, must understand Illinois and Iowa. New England is, indeed, dwarfed in the larger life of the mellower regions of the Republic. It may be the taunt of her enemies, that hers is a departed sceptre, is substantially true; but she has a resurrection here, and her sons and daughters have come to a new glory in these prairies, heavenly by comparison with her sterile hillsides. Stop and see if you recognize them in their new robes.

Council Bluffs, the depot of the gathering lines of the East, and Omaha, opposite, the starting-point of the grand continental line, challenge attention for the striking diversity and yet striking similarity of their locations on the bottoms and bluffs of the Missouri River, as well as for the wonderful rapidity of their growth and their large future promise. Four railroads come in already from the East at Council Bluffs; very soon the number will be doubled; and with these and the swift and strong Missouri rolling between, and carrying steamboats two thousand miles north to the very line of British America and the Rocky Mountains, and two thousand miles south to the Gulf of Mexico, the two towns are surely to be one of the largest centres of traffic and travel on the continent.

We shall not need to stop for the next five

hundred miles. The first hundred and fifty are a repetition of the Iowa we have left behind, — rich rolling prairies, already broken by plough, or smoothed with the track of the mower, — beyond, the grand Plains proper, cut by the Platte, with wood-houses and water-spouts every twelve or fifteen miles, and workshops and eating-houses every seventy-five or one hundred; the road straight as an arrow across the whole region, and apparently as level as the floor, though actually rising steadily at the rate of ten feet to the mile for the entire five hundred miles; there is enough of the ride over it to satisfy curiosity and exhaust its novelty, — there is none too much to absorb the grand impressions of vastness, and majesty of area, and take in the glory of sunset and sunrise along the unending horizon. The Plains introduce us, also, to that dry, pure atmosphere — that cloudless sky and far-reaching vision — which is the great and growing charm of the whole region from the Missouri River to the Pacific

Ocean. Moving westward from New England, there is a constantly increasing dryness of atmosphere, with a broadening sweep and power for the eye; but, after getting fairly outside Eastern influences upon the Plains, it takes on a positive presence, and the traveller feels it as a beauty, as an exhilaration, an inspiration to every sense. It surrounds him with a new world; it infects him with a new spirit; and it hangs the banners of pleasure and of beauty over experiences and upon forms that never would have borne them under different skies and in a denser atmosphere. The nights become cold also. Glaring as may have been the day's sun, and searching its heat, the evening brings refreshing coolness, and the night need of blankets. This phenomenon, too, will attend him through all the new countries he is now entering upon.

At Cheyenne the Plains end and the Mountains begin — in the eye of faith and the figures of railroad subsidies. The hills at least come into sight, and though the track goes forward through an open country, the shadows of the great Rocky Mountain belt fall faintly around us. Cheyenne wondered and waited long, but finally determined to be a town. Colorado makes its connection here with the continental road; it is as high up — near six thousand feet above the sea level — as that road will care to have the winter quarters of its supplies and machinery; it is far enough away to be out of the shadow of Omaha, and Denver lies one hundred miles to the south, and is off the main route. So the town has several thousand settled population, and is steadily growing.

But here we must switch off the main track. We must see Denver, the real Rocky Mountains, which the railroad cheats us of, their grand snow peaks and their wonderful wide parks, the scene and the source of the central life of the continent, before we shall talk with the Mormons, hear the sigh of the Sierra Nevada pines, or listen to the roll of the Pacific waters.

III.

COLORADO.

THOUGH Colorado lies below the line of our first Pacific Railroad, and above the second, which I take it will be the southern, she cannot be refused a first place among their revelations. Because of her mountains, which turn the tracks north and south, she allures the lovers of the grand and picturesque in scenery; because of her mines of gold and silver, she seduces the greedy for gain; because of the agricultural resources of her plains and her valleys, she will have steady growth, permanent prosperity, and moral rectitude, for these are the gifts of a recompensing soil; because of her many and various mineral springs, soda, sulphur, and iron, and of her wonderfully clear, dry, and pure atmosphere, she will be the resort of the health-seeking. Within her borders the great continental mountains display their most magnificent proportions, the great continental rivers spring from melting snows, the plains most warmly invite the farmer and the husbandman, and the best population, between the Missouri River and California, has organized itself into a State. Fifty thousand people here have more than become self-supporting; they are already wealth-producing; and social order and its institutions of education and religion are established. The main Pacific Railroad wisely hastens to connect itself with them by a branch from Cheyenne to Denver; and St. Louis "builded better than she knew," after all, when, in the apparent spirit of a blind rivalry, she pushed her Eastern Division Pacific Road straight towards their centre. Failing to go through the mountains, this road will yet find recompense in furnishing the most direct communication between Colorado and the East, and in throwing out branches from its terminus here, through the best agricultural sections of Colorado, to the main continental lines above and below.

If the branch track is not laid to Denver when we leave Cheyenne, so much the better. The stage ride of this one hundred miles is an experience to which I welcome the stranger. It is the best representation of that sort of travel which the rapid progress of our railway system has left us. Fine Concord coaches, six sleek and gay horses in every team, changed each ten miles, good meals on the way, the road itself generally smooth and hard over the open, rolling prairie, the sky clear, the air an inspiration, the open ocean of the plains on one side, the long and high mountain battlements shadowing us on the other, — altogether, this is as fine a bit of out-door life, by day, as will come within the range of all our summer's journey. By night — for the ride covers the night, as well — new elements come in, which I forbear to detail; but if my companions served in the war, or have tended sick and cross babies through a winter's night, when they had the toothache themselves, I am sure they will survive it.

We shall like Denver, spread out upon the rising plain, with the Platte River flowing through and around it, with broad streets and fine blocks of stores, and a panoramic mountain view before it, such as rises before no other town in all the circle of modern travel. For one hundred miles, buttressed on the north by Long's Peak, and on the south by Pike's Peak, each over fourteen thousand feet high, its line of majestic rock and snow peaks stretches before the eye, ever a surprise by its variety, ever a beauty by its form and color, ever an inspiration in its grandeur. The Alps from Berne do not compare with the Rocky Mountains from Denver; in nearness, in variety, in clearness of atmosphere, in grand sweep of distance, in majestic uplifting of height, these are vastly the superior. Any man with a susceptibility to God's presence in nature must find it very easy to be good in Denver. Certainly, to watch these mountains through the changes of light and cloud of a summer's day and evening is a joyful experience, worth coming from a long distance to Denver to share.

The mining centres of Colorado are up among its mountains, twenty-five, fifty, and seventy-five miles from Denver, which is but the political and business capital, and thus facilities exist for travel into the regions whither we would go for knowledge and joy of nature. Ten hours of staging take us through Central City, the chief gold-mining centre, at a height of seven thousand feet above the sea, with a population of several thousands, on to Georgetown, two thousand feet higher, the centre of the silver production, with nearly three thousand inhabitants. The way is full of mountain and valley scenery of freshest interest and majestic beauty. At Idaho and Fall River, little villages in the South Clear Creek valley, on the route, are accommodations for summer visitors, with cold and warm soda springs at the former place, furnishing most luxurious bathing. And at Georgetown, with larger and better hotels, we are in the very centre of the highest and finest mountain life in the State.

Gray's Peaks, the highest explored summits of Colorado (14,300 and 14,500 feet high), and named for the distinguished Cambridge botanist, lie just beyond and above the town, and the excursion to and from their tops may easily be made in a day with guide and horses from Georgetown. The working of mines up as high as twelve thousand feet has secured a wagon-road two thirds the way, and trails for horses lead to the two summits of the mountain. The view from either of a clear morning is the most commanding and impressive, I truly believe, within the range of all ordinary American or European travel. Nothing in the Alps takes you so high, reaches so wide. There we overlook a petty province; here the broad American continent spreads itself around us as a centre, and stretches out its illimitable lengths before the eye. The rain-drops falling on one coat sleeve flow off to the Pacific, on the other, to the Atlantic. We are at the very apex, the absolute physical centre, of the North American continent; the scene assures the thought, and is worthy of the fact. Fold on fold of snow-slashed and rock-ribbed mountains lie all around, — west, east, north, and south; they riot in luxuriant multiplicity; for this is the fastness, the gathering and distributing point of the grand continental range; while away to the east lies the gray-green sea of the plains, and distributed among the snow-folds of the mountains are miniature copies of the same, which look like patches of prairie amid the continent of mountains, yet are, in fact, great Central Parks, from ten to thirty miles wide and forty to seventy miles long. North, Middle, South, and San Luis Parks, — they lie along through the whole line of central Colorado, — great elevated basins or plains, directly under the highest mountains, — soft and smooth ways upon the very backbone of the continent. Some lie on the Atlantic side, others on the Pacific side of the divide; and their height above the sea level ranges from seven thousand to ten thousand feet. In Europe or in New England this height in this latitude would be perpetual barrenness, more likely perpetual ice and snow; but here in Western America grains and vegetables are successfully cultivated, and cattle graze the year round at seven thousand feet, while between that and ten thousand feet there is rich summer pasturage, and often great crops of natural grass are cured for hay.

These great fertile areas among the high mountains of Colorado — this wedding of majestic hill and majestic plain, of summer and winter, of fecund life and barren rock — present abundant attractions for a full summer's travel. For the lover of the grand and the novel in nature, or the weary seeking rest from toil and excitement, our country offers nothing so richly recompensing as a summer among the parks and mountains of Colorado. The dryness of the climate, inviting to out-door life, is favorable to lung difficulties, though the very thin air of the higher regions must be avoided by those whose lungs are quite weak. Asthma and bronchitis flee before the breath of this dry, pure atmosphere, and it operates as an exhilarating nerve-tonic to all. Denver and St. Louis are about in the same latitude, and their thermometers have nearly the same range, though Denver is nearly six thousand feet higher. Its noons are probably warmer, as its nights are certainly cooler, the year round; but the drier and lighter air, ever in motion from plain and mountain, makes its summer heats always tolerable. Denver is exposed to snow from October to May, but it rarely stays long; sleighing is as much of a novelty as at Washington or Philadelphia, and its winters are more like a dry, clear New England November than any other season of the East. The valleys and parks of the mountains are similar in climactic character, with the added influences of three or four thousand feet greater elevation. The principal snows are in early spring, and the rains in late spring and early summer. Midwinter and midsummer are uniformly dry and clear. When clouds and storms do come, they are always brief. The sun soon shines through them to warm and clear the sky.

The saddle and the camp are the true conditions of extended travel or a summer's life in Colorado. A party of four, well-mounted on mules or Western ponies, with a guide and servant, and two pack-mules for tents and blankets and food, can gain such experience of rare nature, such gift of health, such endowment of pleasure, in leisurely travel over its mountains and among its parks, lingering by the side of their beautiful lakes and their abundant streams fat with trout, basking in its sunshine, hunting in its woods, and bathing in its mineral springs, as nowhere else that I know of in all America. This is surely destined to be "the correct thing to do" for the pleasure and health seekers of the future America.

Over in Middle Park, two days' horseback ride from Georgetown, are the famous Hot Sulphur

Springs, a douche-bath and a sitz-bath united, such as only experience of their wondrous tonic can appreciate. The water is of the temperature of 110° Fahrenheit, — as hot as human flesh can bear, — and pours over a ledge of rock ten feet high into a pool below with a stream of four to six inches in diameter. When wagon-roads are made to the spot, as they soon will be, invalids will flock to these springs in July and August from the whole country. Already they are a favorite local resort, despite the hard climb over the mountains into the valley where they lie.

The South Park is the most attractive and most frequented of these elevated park areas; and a good wagon-road from Denver, branching out within the park to all its various sections, and taverns and mining villages strung freely along one and through the other, invite the traveller to its easy enjoyment. Mount Lincoln, the great parent mountain of the parent range, stands at the northwestern angle of the park, and may be ascended without too severe labor from the village of Montgomery. It is of nearly or quite the same height as Gray's Peaks, and commands a like view. The connoisseurs in mountain views in Colorado dispute as to which summit offers the wider and grander. Either is grand enough, and one or other should be enjoyed by every visitor to Colorado. Our ascent of Lincoln was made amid contending torrents of rain, snow, hail, and sunshine, and though the views we obtained were not so complete and satisfactory as those from Gray, the experience was perhaps the grander, because of its variety, and the terrible impressiveness of a storm on the mountain-tops, opening and closing long glimpses of ghastly worlds of rocks and snow below and all around us.

The upper mountains of Colorado — at eleven thousand and twelve thousand feet — hold numerous pools and lakes, and not infrequent waterfalls. A party who made the ascent of Long's Peak for the first time, last season, report nearly forty lakes in view at once; but the parks and lower ranges offer them but rarely. A day's ride, in saddle or wagon, out of South Park, over into the valley of the Upper Arkansas, — where various new beauties of scenery await the explorer, — will carry us into the presence of the Twin Lakes, as beautifully lying sheets of water as mountains ever guarded or sun illuminated. They hold kinship with the Cumberland lakes of England, the Swiss and Italian lakes, and those of Tahoe and Donner in the California Sierra Nevada, which are among the sweet revelations of the Pacific Railroad. The Twin Lakes will be one of the specialties when the world goes to Colorado for its summer vacations.

The tree life of the Rocky Mountains is meagre; pines and firs and aspens (or cottonwood) make up its catalogue; nor are these so abundant or so rich in size or beauty as to challenge special attention. They grow in greatest luxuriance at elevations of from eight to eleven thousand feet; and the timber line does not cease till nearly twelve thousand feet is reached. A silver fir or spruce is the one charm among the trees. But the flora is more varied and more beautiful; Dr. Parry reports one hundred and forty-one different species in these higher mountains, eighty-four of which are peculiar to them; and I can report that nowhere else have I gathered such wealth — in glory of color and perfection and numbers — of fringed gentians, harebells, painter's brush, buttercups, larkspurs, child sunflowers, dandelions, and columbines, as on these eight and ten thousand feet high hillsides, or in little nooks of grass and grove still higher. Blue and yellow are the dominant colors; but the reds flame out in the painter's brush and the kernel of the sunflowers, like beacons of light amid darkness. With much lacking in details of beauty and interest, that are found in the country life of New England and the Middle States, as in California, Colorado more than redeems herself by the charm of her atmosphere and the magnificent majesty of her mountains and her plains. These are her title to supremacy, her claim to be to America what Switzerland is to Europe.

But I cannot hope my Pacific Railroad travellers will give more than seven or ten days to Colorado, — an appetizer for a future summer's feast, — and I rely on the patriotic and thrifty citizens of Denver and Georgetown to perfect some arrangements by which, in that time, they may get a fair glimpse of its grand and rare specialties of mountain ranges and enfolded parks, and a share in the out-door life they invite. A ride up through the mountains by Boulder Creek or South Clear Creek valleys, on to the head of the latter above Empire or at Georgetown, the ascent of Gray or Lincoln, and a peep into and a cut across the South Park, with two or three nights in camp, and a half-day's trout-fishing, — these I consider essential; and under good guidance they may all be had within the time mentioned. Ascending Gray's Peaks from Georgetown, I should recommend going down on the other side, and a night's camp on the Snake River; thence to the junction of the Snake, the Blue, and Ten

Mile Creek; up the Blue to Breckinridge; over the Breckinridge Pass into South Park at Hamilton or Fairplay; and thence, if there is not time for Lincoln or the Arkansas Lakes, across the Park and out to Denver by Turkey Creek Canyon and the Plains. All this could be put into seven days from Denver, though ten would be better; but, through lack of a wagon-road from Georgetown over to Snake River, it would have to be done in part or altogether in the saddle. Hotels could be reached for all but one or two nights; but these may be made, with fortunate camping-ground, choice, companions, and plenty of blankets and firewood, the most memorable and happy of the whole week.

With such experience as this, we go back to the railroad at Cheyenne, with a new sense of the greatness of America, with a curious doubting wonder as to what can lie beyond, and with appetites that we shall probably have to go to Ford's to satisfy, while waiting for our train for Salt Lake City.

IV.

THE MOUNTAINS AND THE MORMONS.

RESUMING the cars, for the grand ride over the Rocky Mountain section of the track, an hour or so from Cheyenne takes us to Sherman, the highest point (8,200 feet) of the entire railroad line. But we feel rather than see the evidences of the fact. The air is thin and chill, even under a July or August sun; but it is a high plain, and not mountain-tops, that the track rests upon. There are bare, smoothly-rounded hills about; scattered over them are huge boulders, or piles of boulders, like remnants of mountains; but the mountains themselves stand far away in the dim distance; and the train speeds free and nearly straight over an open and comparatively level country, crossing an occasional deep ravine or river-bed, cutting through a rare rock remnant of the original hilltops, but altogether finding easy pathway through the one hundred and fifty miles that counted, in the government subsidy, as peculiarly the mountainous section, and had the exceptional allowance of $48,000 a mile. A clean reddish granite, ground fine by nature, makes the most compact and enduring of road-beds; the ties come from thin forests in the distant hills; and altogether we are still in a paradise for railroad contractors.

Down and on from Sherman a thousand feet and twenty-five miles the land grows more level still, and the Laramie Plains spread a broad fifty miles around us. They are like one of the parks below in Colorado, only the mountains do not lie so close and commanding around, and the views are less picturesque and nature less rich; but the neighboring hills will repay the sportsman. A considerable village is springing up at Laramie; the Plains are famous in overland emigrant travel, and were long headquarters for the government supplies and soldiers in the mountains; and those of us who failed to look into the parks of Colorado will be well repaid for stopping here a day or two.

Beyond, the country grows gradually barren; and after crossing the North Platte River, we enter upon one hundred and fifty miles of desert, — a waterless, treeless, grassless, rolling plain, the soil fine, dry, and impregnated with alkali, the air pure, dry, and cool, — a section shudderingly remembered by slow-travelling emigrants, and memorable in the history of railroad construction for the necessity of having a special water train to supply the workmen and the engines while carrying forward the work through it. Rightly named Bitter Creek gathers the sluggish surface waters it furnishes, and carries them on to Green River, reaching which we enter upon new and better scenes. The water increases and freshens, the verdure improves; but that which attracts the traveller most is the novel and imposing forms of architecture that Nature has left to mark her history upon these still open plains. Long, wide troughs, as of departed rivers; long level embankments, as of railroad tracks or endless fortifications; huge, quaint hills, suddenly rising from the plain, bearing fantastic shapes; great square mounds of rock and earth, half-formed, half-broken pyramids, — it would seem as if a generation of giants had built and buried here, and left their work to awe and humble a puny succession. The Black, the Pilot, and the Church *Buttes* are among the more celebrated of these huge monumental mountains standing on the level plain; but the railway track passes out of sight of them all except the Church Butte, which, seen under favorable lights, imposes on the imagination like a grand old cathedral going into decay, quaint in its crumbling ornaments, majestic in its height and breadth. They seem, like the more numerous and fantastic illustrations of Nature's frolicsome art in Southern Colorado, to be the remains of granite hills that wind and water, and especially the sand whirlpools which march in lordly force through the air, — literally moving mountains, — have left to hint the past, and tell the story of their own achievements. Not unfitly, there as here, they have won the title of "Monuments to the Gods."

Passing the waters that flow south to the Colorado, we come to those that run west to the Salt Lake Basin. Nature now deserts us as a railroad engineer; and high art and mighty labor are summoned to make a path for the track through and down these western ranges of the Rocky Mountains. Over and down the high hills, the road at last reaches Echo Canyon, and, following that to its entrance into Weber Canyon, proceeds by this into the Valley of the Salt Lake. These canyons are narrow and rugged, with high, perpendicular walls of red rock, with picturesque openings and fresh running streams, with little Mormon farms, and every element of agreeable and inspiring scenery. The mountain-tops are white with snow; the valleys are green with grass or gay with flowers; and those greatly cherished but long-missed companions of man, the trees, now come in to freshen and familiarize the scene. Within this region we meet, moving west, the first tunnels of the road; and there are five of them, aggregating nearly two thousand feet, between Green River and the Salt Lake Valley.

Our travellers across the continent, men or women, will not need urging to stop at Salt Lake City, though it lies forty miles south of Ogden, where the Pacific Railroad enters and crosses the Salt Lake Valley. The social and the natural phenomena centring there make it perhaps the most interesting feature in our journey. The courage of men who undertake the management of numberless wives will attract one sex, while the audacity of the act will arouse the wonder, if not the worship, of the other. Here, too, are study for the statesman, thought for the philosopher, and puzzles for the scientific student. But the science of Salt Lake City, social and natural, presents problems not easily solved; and one must be content to look upon the surface of things, and move on. There will be, this summer, a branch railroad to the city, and sooner or later the track will proceed on south through the lower Mormon settlements to Arizona.

The town will delight us with its location, on a high plain over the broad valley of the Jordan, Camp Douglas behind on a higher bench of land, the Wahsatch Mountains, with winter caps, hanging above it on the north and east, while opposite lower mountains make a western horizon, and Salt Lake, an inland ocean, ripples and shimmers under the noonday sun, fifteen miles away. Broad streets, with the irrigating brooks pouring down their gutters; good hotels; large and well-supplied stores; an abundant market; a large and well-appointed theatre, run in the name and for the benefit of the Church; gardens luxurious with fruit, the peach and the strawberry most abounding, and bountiful with vegetables; hot sulphur springs in the suburbs, inviting most luxurious baths; summer days, dry and pure, yet cool nights, — all these will seduce the senses and minister to our joy, and the traveller may well sing with Bishop Heber that "every prospect pleases, and only man is vile." A drive out to Salt Lake, and a bath and a sail, if they are to be had, guarding the mouth and eyes from the water, which is sharply salt, and the stomach from sea-sickness, for the wind makes short waves on this sea; an attendance, if it is Sunday, — and we should manage to have our visit cover a Sabbath, — upon the services in the grand Church Square, where we shall see the old and new tabernacles, and the foundations of the grand Mormon cathedral, as well as an audience of several thousand Mormons, affording an interesting human study; a walk under the high wall around Brigham Young's equally grand square opposite, with tithing-house, home for thirty wives and seventy children, private school-house for the family, all the central business offices of church and state, stables and warehouses to match so mammoth an establishment, and gardens of grapes and peaches and pears and flowers and vegetables, all within the area, — counting up, as we walk, the contending passions and conflicting experiences, the crushed loves and the subdued hates, the moral murders perpetrated, the physical murders planned, enfolded in this ten-acre circuit of wall; an excursion back to the mouth of the canyon that overlooks city and valley; a numbering of the front-doors of the long, low adobe cottages, as the simplest means of learning how many wives each owner has, and wondering if half of these children, that swarm in every door-yard, and play around every mud-puddle, have any idea who their fathers are, — these embrace all that such passing travellers can hope or need to see and experience of Utah and the Mormons; and for these from two to four days will suffice.

We shall busy ourselves, of course, with a dozen questions and a dozen theories about Mormonism, about polygamy and Brigham Young, and when and how they are all coming to an end; perhaps, if we hear earnest Mormons talk, we shall wonder in our hearts if it is possible they are right, and this little leaven in Utah is, as they say, bound to leaven the whole American lump, and polygamy become the law of the sexes, and Mormonism the religion of the future, — which is all well enough if we keep our wondering doubts to ourselves. We may know, if we observe closely and think intelligently, that no social, political, and religious organization, all bound into one and proceeding from a common head, so foreign to all our principles of life and growth, as this of Brigham Young in Utah, exists elsewhere in America, nor even in Europe, indeed; and it will take but little knowledge of history and its philosophy, and less of the American instinct of life and of man's progress, to convince us that it must give way, and be swept almost into forgetfulness by the advancing tide of American emigration and American civilization. There is nothing in our American fundamentals that is not outraged in the theories and practice of the autocracy that rules here in Utah; and unless we are going speedily back to the civilization of Abraham, Isaac, and Jacob, this thing will not be, cannot be. And yet a beautiful and prosperous city of twenty-five thousand inhabitants, and a surrounding territory of near one hundred thousand, making a garden here in the dry desert of this central basin of the continent, will impress us wonderfully, as it ought, with the power of a religious fanaticism, directed by a lordly will, and organizing a faithful, simple industry, to create wealth, and to set in motion many of the elements of progress and civilization. But for the pioneership of the Mormons, discovering the pathway, and feeding those who came out upon it, all this central region of our great West would be now many years behind its present development, and the railroad, instead of being finished, would hardly be begun.

V.

FROM SALT LAKE TO THE PACIFIC.

THERE is no end to the anomalies of nature in this great interior American basin, of which the Salt Lake Valley is alike the threshold, the gem, and a sub-specimen. But the study of them is now accompanied with so many drawbacks that the pleasure-traveller will, after leaving Salt Lake City, seek to put the whole region between him and the Sierras as speedily as possible. Ascending and passing out of the Valley, the road skirts the northern shore of the lake, crossing Bear River, its chief tributary, and going through the Promontory Mountains that come down from the north into the lake. Here the two companies building the railroad, from east and west, joined their tracks, though the point of actual connection is at Ogden, in the valley below; from here the stage lines start, northeast and northwest, to Montana and Idaho; and from here, too, the Union or Eastern Pacific company intends to stretch a branch road up to and along the Snake branch of the Columbia River, through Idaho, and down the Columbia to the sea, thus making for itself a distinct connection with the Pacific Ocean. The distance is six hundred and fifty miles, but for half of it steamboats can run on the rivers, so that the first construction, to insure steam communication, is comparatively not large, and will hardly require more money than the profits of the company in building the main line.

Stretching out from Salt Lake through high broad valleys or plains, barren and forbidding, the road seeks the Humboldt Valley, and follows that river for two hundred and thirty miles. This is the old emigrant route across the continent, cheerless and dreary enough, indeed, but far more tolerable than the old stage-road, which led us south of Salt Lake, and crossed Nevada at about its centre. The river is sluggish and muddy, and fertilizes but a narrow strip of land in its path; it lies along a trough between high volcanic table-lands on the north, and the ranges of mountains that every fifteen or twenty miles lead off south through Nevada, and out of whose snows it gathers its feeble waters. Where the road enters the valley wide and watery meadows spread out a sickly oasis, and where it leaves it the same phenomenon is repeated; for the rest, there is little to divert the traveller, nothing to inspire him but the dry, clear air, and the rounded outlines of the bare hills. Elko, where the main tributary of the Humboldt comes out of the snow-capped East Humboldt mountains, which are ten thousand to twelve thousand feet high, and the backbone of the great basin, is the point of departure for the new silver-mines of White Pine, the latest sensation of the sensation-loving Pacific coast. They lie one hundred and forty miles south of the railroad, in Southeastern Nevada, and if they hold out as they have begun, with a pretty sure promise of five millions the first year, they will force the first southern cross railroad to the Colorado, and checkmate Mormonism in the south.

A little farther out we touch a bit of emigrant sentiment in Maggie Creek from the north, so named for a pretty little Scotch girl, pet of one of the early columns of the army of civilization crossing this way years ago. Here is Carlin, a town of hopes, as marking a point of departure from the West for Idaho. Near here, too, if the locomotive breaks down, the traveller may refresh himself by climbing a little knob, a few rods from the road, and find that nature has improved an old crater by turning it into a mammoth hot sulphur bath-tub. At Argenta he will be invited to a stage ride of ninety miles up the Reese River valley to Austin; but if he has ever invested in any of its mines, he will decline with a shudder, and set his face resolutely west. The glory of Austin is a trifle dimmed now; but it has had its five or six thousand inhabitants, and was the successor of "Washoe," and the forerunner of White Pine, in the series of mining movements that have made Nevada, and even threaten to perpetuate her existence as a State against every other Divine gift and grace.

If we are bent on novelty, eighteen miles farther west we shall switch off our car for half a day, and borrow horses and gallop away south, among the barren hills and more barren valleys, into the Whirlwind Valley, where sulphurous waters beat and bubble beneath the surface, like numerous struggling hidden pumps or steam-engines, and occasionally burst out in columns of burning water and clouds of hot steam. Great, still pools invite to a bath, yet mayhap would overtake the bather with a scalding, crystallizing explosion, and leave him a monumental statue of his temerity, and a new wonder of Nature in the Great Basin. Frequently she revenges herself here for her stint in all the ordinary natural graces by these deposits of seething chemicals, that seem to be faint breathings of dying volcanoes, or the early efforts of new ones.

Passing between the Trinity Mountains on the north and the West Humboldt on the south, and through a mining district of great hopes, large prospecting, and small returns, the road now leaves the Humboldt River, which sneaks off among the hills to die in the sands, and, crossing the Truckee Desert, forty miles of the dreariest country it has yet passed, — arid, alkalish, and Arabic, the only life, lizards and jackass rabbits, the only landscape feature, dry, brown, and bare mountains, the only hope, the end, — the track brings us within the waters and the winds of the California mountains.

Along the Truckee to Reno, we should there take a day to see Virginia City and Gold Hill, fourteen miles away on a branch road. The great Comstock lode lies under these two towns; they are built along the mountain-side, upon the crust of the great silver-mine of America, with open depths beneath of from five hundred to one thousand feet, and more miles of streets below than above; and they are the theatre of the most systematic and extensive if not the most successful mining operations in this country. The mines in this lode have yielded over eighty millions in gold and silver since 1860,.reaching sixteen millions, or their highest year's return, in 1867, but falling off one half in 1868, and giving signs now of being nearly worked out. It is in the hope of their renewal, at least of a more profitable working, that Congress is besought to give millions for a tunnel from far down the valley in under the mountain to the lode at a point below its present excavations. But with any real faith in the future possibilities of the mine, the money for the work can be raised in California and Nevada easier than it can be bored and bought through Congress. The question at issue is one of life or death to these towns; but they are well worth even the hurried traveller's visit, as well for their historical relations to silver-mining, to the settlement and organization of Nevada, and to the Pacific Railroad, as for offering the best opportunity for observing the processes of quartz mining and milling, and not a little, indeed, for the uniqueness of their location and the surrounding natural objects of interest.

The "Steamboat Springs" in the neighborhood repeat the phenomena of Whirlwind Valley. Carson, the capital, lies pleasantly in an adjoining valley nearer the great mountains; but the mountains themselves now invite us more strongly, and we are soon moving swiftly among their gurgling waters and soughing pines, — rarer water and grander forest than we have seen before, — with towering walls of rock and distant snow-fields, that are full of Alpine memories. The snow-sheds over the track shut out the best of the mountain scenery, and we must stop near the summit of Donner Lake, a beautiful sheet of water, already a favorite summer resort for California, and type of a series of grand lakes along the upper Sierras, that add a rare charm to their many other scenic attractions. A day or two here will make us familiar with the numerous beauties of this mountain range, the grand forests, the castellated rocks, the wedded summer and winter, the dry, pure air, the mosses, the flowers and mountain fruits, and refresh us for the descent into the hot suns and the brown valleys of California's summer.

The railroad passage over these mountains is the greatest triumph of engineering skill and labor on the whole line. The track going west ascends twenty-five hundred feet in fifty miles, and descends six thousand feet in seventy-five miles. There are over a mile of tunnels on the route, and a million of dollars were spent in blasting-powder alone for the construction. Majestic, frowning peaks hang over us, deep, almost fathomless gorges lie beneath us, as we follow out and around the long ridges in the descent into California; and amid scenes more bold and impressive than any we have yet passed through, we pass out into the lower valleys, and reach California's capital, Sacramento.

Three lines invite us thence to San Francisco: the river-boats; a short-cut railroad to Vallejo at the head of the bay, with a twenty-mile ferriage; or the Pacific Railroad's proper prolongation around through Stockton to Oakland, the rural suburb and school-house of San Francisco, lying opposite, and an hour's steamboat ride away, on the bay. By and by rails will circuit the bay, and we may go into the heart of San Francisco without " breaking bulk" or touching water. Sacramento, Stockton, and Oakland are all worth a passing glance. They are inland rural cities, like Cleveland and Columbus in Ohio, or Hartford, Springfield, and Worcester in New England, pleasantly located by the water, brisk with local trade and developing manufactures, mature in social and religious elements, rich in many beautiful homes; they rank next to San Francisco among the towns of California. Sacramento and Stockton stand respectively at the heads of the Sacramento and San Joaquin valleys, which form, north and south, the great interior basin and agricultural region of the State, and whose waters uniting pour westward and circle San Francisco with her wealth of bay.

VI.

SAN FRANCISCO.

BUT it is at San Francisco that we shall linger and take in the essence of California life, and cast the future of California's wealth. First we shall go to the Occidental, Cosmopolitan, Russ, or Lick Hotels, and live at three dollars a day, — specie, mind you, now, — as well as at the Tremont or Fifth Avenue. Perhaps we shall have a mind to try that "peculiar institution" of the city, the "What Cheer House," where meals and lodgings are fifty cents each, with a library and natural history and mineralogical museums thrown in; we shall certainly want to test the French restaurants, where, at sharp six and a private table, we may have for a dollar and a half as good a dinner of four or five courses, wine included, as Parker or Delmonico will give us for a five-dollar bill.

The fruit surprise will have been broken to us as we came down from the mountains; but still the wonder grows at the sight of the city fruit-stands,— Sweetwater and Black Hamburg and Muscat grapes at from five to twelve cents a pound, and poorer qualities at half the price; strawberries the season through; peaches and pears, more fair and luscious and large than our senses were ever accustomed to; fresh figs, oranges, limes, and bananas,— all at moderate prices, and all in such abundance on the hotel tables and in the streets as to make a fruit-famished New-Englander rub his eyes and prick his flesh lest he be in a fairy-land dream. Then the more substantial articles of food: here is flour at half Atlantic prices, and vegetables of every kind, spring, summer, and fall varieties, all at once in fullest perfection; here are fresh salmon twelve months in the year, at from ten to twenty cents a pound, and smelts at eight cents, and fresh cod, bass, shrimps, anchovies, soles, even herrings, every treasure of the sea; and game as various, and at prices that in many instances shame our Eastern markets. The materials for living are in as rich supply here as the art of their preparation is perfect, and it will not take the thrifty mind long to calculate that, so far as food is concerned, a family can be supported more cheaply in San Francisco than in New York or Boston. The rates quoted are, of course, specie; but wages and profits are also in specie, and are higher, generally, than currency wages and profits in Eastern cities.

The summer, we must remember, is apt to be chillier than the winter in San Francisco; and though the morning sun may seduce us, it will never do to venture out for the day in shoes and white stockings or without overcoats. Montgomery Street is Wall Street and Broadway united, and at all hours of the day is full of business life and fashionable gayety, — the promenade of richly dressed women, the busy arena of "cornering" and "cornered" men. To the right, chiefly on made land, flat and regular, lie the heavy business squares of the city; to the left we mount, through retail shops to homes, with weary legs and bended backs, the great sand-hills that are such a blessing to street contractors, such a trial to land-owners and tax-payers, yet for us such a grand point of view over city and surroundings, over the wide range of interior waters that gather here from all the State, and, with delaying, lingering movement, circle the city as with a sea, and then reluctantly and yet with majestic sweep pass through the line of rocks by the Golden Gate into the Ocean. We must be sure and get this grand view of city and bay from several points; it is a revelation in itself of the future Pacific Coast Empire, certainly of San Francisco's security as its metropolis.

The San Franciscans, having begun wrongly on the American straight line and square system of laying out the city, are tugging away at these hills with tireless energy, to reduce the streets to a grade that man and horse can ascend and descend without double collar and breeching help; but there is work in it for many a generation to come. They would have done better in accepting the situation at the first, chosen Nature engineer and architect in chief, and circled the hills with their streets and buildings, instead of undertaking to go up and then through them. Such a flank attack would have been much more successful and economical and given them a vastly more picturesque city.

In town, the buildings of the Mercantile and Young Men's Christian Associations, and of the California Bank, the financial king of the coast, will attract us; the school-houses and churches will show that New England has been aggressive here for years; the machine-shops and woollen-mills will suggest that we talk lower of Lowell and Holyoke and Pittsburg; and the stores and shops and little factories of all sorts, springing into success all about our wandering paths in city and suburbs, will prove to us that here are a people not only capable of going alone, but already doing so. San Francisco is only twenty years old, yet she has one hundred and fifty thousand inhabitants, a third of the population of the whole State; her manufactures aggregate thirty millions a year, which exceeds the gold and silver products of the State, and equals the wheat crop; her commerce employs from forty to fifty steamships and three thousand sailing vessels; and, already the third, she will soon be the second commercial city of the nation. It is not best to burden our soul with many statistics; but if we expect to get along without either a quarrel with or the contempt of our California friends, we must show that we know on what this Cæsar of cities is feeding, and how fat she is sure to be. They talk lovingly as well as grandly of "Frisco" out here, and they only allow New York to be ranked as a rival when they are in their most condescending moods. Boston is where Starr King came from, and that is glory enough for her, and she ought to be forever grateful to California for giving him fit field for his powers, and so renown to his birthplace.

In the clear, quiet morning, before the wind

sucks in over these sand-hills through the Golden Gate, and the coarse dust blinds and stings, we will drive out to the ocean at the Cliff House. It is an hour's ride, and the road is smooth and hard. We might well stop for an hour at Lone Mountain Cemetery, and see how San Francisco is making a fit burial-place, under adverse circumstances, and pays tribute to the memory of Broderick and James King of William, proud martyrs to the political and social reformation of the town and State. On the rocks before the Cliff House, — where we shall take our second breakfast or lunch, — an army of huge seals creep up to sun themselves and bark, and great, gawky pelicans flap about; and, getting down under the bank, we lie on the hard sands, and try to realize that this is the Pacific Ocean, and that beyond lie the Sandwich Islands and China and Japan. Driving back along the hard beach for miles, our horses trotting to the roll of the ocean, we attack the city from another quarter, see its proud

Orphan Asylum, its old Mission grounds, and appreciate how much room for growth these wide-rolling sand-hills afford.

The ever-present Chinese will pique our curiosity. We must look into their homes, compact, simple, yet not over clean or sweet-smelling quarters, into their restaurants, and their theatre, if it is open, and into their "Josh Houses." Their stores invite us with open doors, and tempt our pockets with all the various specialties of Chinese manufacture at reasonable prices. The few are men of stature and presence, with faces of refinement and gentle strength; the many go sneaking about their work, a low type of man, physically and mentally, that are imported here like merchandise, and let out to labor under a system only half removed from slavery itself. But they are an important element in the industry and progress of all this side of the continent. Except for their labor, the Pacific Railroad would have been at least two years longer in building. Twelve thousand of them have done nearly all the picking and drilling and shovelling and wheeling of the road from Sacramento to Salt Lake. They furnish the principal labor in the factories; they make cigars; they dig and work over neglected gold-gulches; they are cooks; they count the specie in the banks; they almost monopolize the clothes washing and ironing; in all the lighter and simpler departments of labor, where fidelity to a pattern, and not flexibility and originality of action are required, they make the best and most reliable of workers. At least seventy-five thousand of them are scattered over these Pacific States west of Utah; and though our American and European laborers quarrel with and abuse them; though the law gives them no rights but that of suffering punishment; though they bring no families, and seek no citizenship; though all the Chinese women here are not only commercial, but expressly imported as such; though they are mean and contemptible in their vices as in their manners; though they are despised and kicked about on every hand, — still they come and thrive, slowly better their physical and moral and mental conditions, and supply this country with the greatest necessity for its growth and prosperity, — cheap labor. What we shall do with them is not quite clear yet; how they are to rank — socially, civilly, and politically — among us, is one of the nuts for our social science students to crack, — if they can; but now that we have depopulated Ireland, and Germany is holding on to its own, and so the old sources of our labor supply are drying up, all America needs them, and, obeying the great natural law of demand and supply, Asia seems almost certain to pour upon and over us countless thousands of her superfluous, cheap-living, slow-changing, unassimilating, but very useful laborers. And we shall welcome, and then quarrel over and with them, as we have done with their Irish predecessors. Our vast grain, cotton, and fruit fields; our extending system of public works; our multiplying system of manufactures, all need and can employ them. But must they vote, and if so, to what effect?

The garden-yards of San Francisco homes, as of other California towns, welcomed us lovingly, and will bid us a sweet adieu. Great open conservatories, with daily artificial waterings in summer, they maintain freshness of color and vigor of bloom the whole year through. Roses of every name and variety, never dying and never resting; heliotropes and fuchsias climbing over fences and houses, — in fact, all our New England June to October blooms make perpetual summer gayety of color and gratefulness of odor, at little outlay of means, around every individual house. The climate of the city is more even than of the country, — never so warm, never so cold; not soft or kind to invalids, but a tonic and a preservative for the well, and keeping labor up to its fullest capacity for the whole twelvemonth.

Let us look into Wells, Fargo, & Co.'s express on Montgomery Street, before we leave San Francisco, for an illustration of how much more thoroughly these new people on the Pacific coast meet the exacting wants of our civilization than either Europe or the Eastern States. Here, for ten cents (three to the Government for the permission and seven for the work), your letter is taken and carried anywhere on the broad continent, delivered, if its direction bears a local habitation and a name, and mailed in the nearest post-office, if it has not; here you can ship merchandise, small or great, to any known spot on the globe's surface; here you can buy gold or greenbacks; here draw on your Eastern correspondents, and receive the cash down; here they will bargain to carry anything for you anywhere, yourself included; to bring you anything, send for anything, sell you anything, supply you with information on any given topic; and generally set you up in knowledge, money, business, and character. Our Eastern express companies never began to make themselves half so useful or omnipresent.

San Francisco will impress all her visitors deeply

in many ways. We see it is very new; yet we see it is very old. Civilization is better organized here in some respects than in any other city except Paris; some of its streets look as if transplanted from a city of Europe; others are in the first stages of rescue from the barbaric desert. Asia, Europe, and America have here met and embraced each other; yet the mark of America is over and upon all; an America in which the flavor of New England can be tasted above all other local elements; an America in which the flexibility, the adaptability, and the all-penetrating, all-subduing power of its own race are everywhere and in everything manifest.

VII.

CALIFORNIA AT LARGE.

OUTSIDE of San Francisco California has many a choice wonder in nature, many a rare development of industry to show its visitors. But summer tourists may be choice in their selections. A few days for railroad excursions into the valleys of the coast mountains about San Francisco will show us some of the grand wheat-fields, the orchards, and the vineyards; will exhibit the advantages of an agriculture that can begin ploughing and planting in December, keep them up till April, and then begin to harvest, and keep at that till October, with no barns necessary for housing animals or crops; will open to us beautiful natural groves of oaks; will reveal to us charming little nooks of rural homes among the adjoining hills; will invite us to health-giving sulphur-baths and soda-springs more delightfully located than Sharon or Saratoga; will give us a peep into the gardens of the old Catholic missionaries among the Indians, now overgrown with peach, plum, and fig trees, where we may have the novelty of picking the ripe figs from trees nearly as large as the big elms on Boston Common; will — if we go far enough — a two days' ride — take us into the wild valley of the Geysers, where a miniature hell sends up its sulphurous waters, and burns and poisons all the earth and air within its reach, and where you peer into each crevice and around every corner in sure faith of seeing the Monster of Evil switching his tail in vengeful activity; again will carry us into the grand forests of redwood in the coast mountains, — sponsor and promise of the mammoth trees of the Sierras, — a light, delicate, reddish cedar that enters largely into the lumber supply of the San Francisco market; will introduce our curious steps to the great quicksilver mine of New Almaden, the rival of the Almaden mine of Spain; or will set us down under the mountains by the ocean's shore at Santa Cruz, the Nice of our Pacific coast, where the pure air breathes soft and low, and invalids rejoice in relief. Farther down, Los Angelos invites us, with stories of the tropical wealth of Southern California, of grape-vines as trees, of orange and olive, of lemon and banana groves, of cotton plantations, of agricultural wealth unbounded, of a climate so dry and even, so soft and sweet, as to surpass Italy's.

But most of us will wait for the Southern Pacific Railroad, already moving out from both sides, to introduce us to this latter region of almost fabulous wealth and beauty; and, after a hasty run, with wide-open eyes, into Napa, Sonoma, and Santa Clara valleys, perhaps into that of Russian River, we shall prepare for the one great wonder which we came out to see, — the Yosemite Valley. For this, ten days, a full purse, and Professor Whitney's new and model guide-book and maps, one of the best incidental gifts of the geological survey of the State, — these and a camping suit, with duster and overcoat, are essential. The best way to go is by night boat or early morning cars to Stockton; and then by stage one hundred miles up the San Joaquin valley, — O how dry and dusty! — through rich wheat-fields, into and through, too, that magnificent ruin, that football of Wall Street, Fremont's Mariposa estate. In one of the dying villages of this principality, Bear Valley or Mariposa, saddle-horses and guides are procured. If possible, add tents, blankets, and food, and travel independent of ranches or hotels. The first day, after leaving the stage, and going up into the mountains, we shall reach White and Hatch's for dinner, to which point we may, if we choose, ride in wagons, and get to Clark's ranch for supper. Here we shall wish, of course, to stop over for a day, to see the Big Trees of the Mariposa Grove. These are four or five miles' distance from Clark's, and, if possible, we persuade him to go with us. He is the State's agent for the care of the Yosemite Valley and the Grove, and a genuine child of the great nature around him;

and whether within his wide-spreading cabins, or under his protecting haystack, or in your own tent by the side of his grand open-air fires, he will care for us as father for children, and be proud to have us praise his trees, his river, and his mountains.

Another day — the fourth — takes us into the grand Valley, after a hundred miles of wagon and forty of saddle riding from Stockton; every man and woman of us making sure to dwell long upon the first views that are opened to us as we come out of the woods, and look over into the depths below, and on to the heights above and beyond. Only seeing is believing what this gorge in the mountains reveals. It is Nature speaking to man in a way that proves and exalts her supremacy. There are simple hotels here; but if we have tents and blankets, we should pass each of our three days and nights at different points in the Valley, one in the lower part, under El Capitan, another where the music of the Yosemite Fall will lull us to sleep, and the third by the lake, or in the neighborhood of the Vernal Fall. All the main features of interest are within a ten-mile line, and the three days will give us ample time to see them comfortably. But these will hold not an hour too much; and no week in any life could be more memorable than the one that should be spent under the rocks and by the side of the waters of the Yosemite.

Another week may be also profitably spent by the lover of rare and majestic nature among the High Sierras circling the Yosemite Valley. Here, upon and among mountains from eight thousand to thirteen thousand feet high, we find beautiful lakes and bright rivers, grand rock and mountain scenery, and a repetition in miniature of the Yosemite Valley itself, called the Hetch-Hetchy Valley; and if we choose to prolong our ride down the Nevada side of the mountains to Mono Lake, we shall discover in that sheet of water, fourteen miles long by nine wide, truly a Sea of Death. No living thing can exist in it; its waters will consume leather, and thoroughly decompose the human body in a few weeks; and though it receives various pure streams from out the mountains, it poisons all from its fountains of death, and, like Salt Lake, has no apparent outlet, and is even more of a puzzle to geologists and chemists than that better known inland sea.

The return trip from the Yosemite should be made by the Coulterville trail and road, keeping our original outfit with us. There are ten miles more of horseback riding on this route; but it introduces us to a change of scenery, and a remarkable cave, called Bower's Cave, and invites us by a short detour to visit the Calaveras Grove of Big Trees, the first discovered and best known of these forest wonders. There are some eight collections of these mammoth trees scattered along the Sierra Mountains within a distance of one hundred and fifty miles; the tallest trees yet measured are full three hundred and twenty-five feet high, and are in the Calaveras collection; and the largest in circumference are in the Mariposa Grove, and measure over ninety feet; while the greatest age that any yet scientifically tested in that respect can claim is about thirteen hundred years. Their beauty of shape and color is as striking as their size; and no visitor to California will omit them in his tour of its curiosities.

Though the mining interests of California have fallen behind those of agriculture and manufactures, and seem destined to still greater decay, there are some features of them decidedly worth a stranger's study. Grass Valley is the centre of the most extensive successful gold quartz mining; and its operations are not dissimilar to those of Central City in Colorado and Virginia City in Nevada. But the disembowelling of the dead rivers of California for the loose deposits of gold left in their beds by the convulsions of nature in ages long past, the deep excavations, and the grand hydraulic processes resorted to for the purpose of reaching them, develop both natural phenomena and great ingenuity and boldness in man, that rank among the curiosities of the State. These dead rivers are not dry, open beds; but huge strata of sand, gravel, and quartz, filling up what were once river channels, and lying now from a hundred to a thousand feet beneath the foot-hills of the mountains. They lie parallel with the Sierra Nevadas, and diagonally to the rivers now coming out of the mountains; they were sponged up and filled up by the upheaval of the hills; and their place was made known by the modern streams cutting down through them, and revealing on the walls of the canyon the peculiar gold-bearing materials that now occupy their beds. Out of these dead rivers three hundred millions in gold have been taken, and they still yield eight millions a year. Much capital and labor are requisite to carry on mining operations in them: tunnels are run along their lines, and great streams of water are brought down from the mountains, through miles of ditches and troughs, and poured, by the aid of hose, with many times more force than the streams from a steam fire-engine, upon a hillside, to tear it to pieces and get at the gold materials, or into the gold-beds themselves to wash out the precious particles. The ruin and waste that such operations spread around are frightful; rivers are choked up with the sands and stones sent down by these washings; and broad valleys of alluvial are made a desert by the overspreading tide of hills they set afloat.

But it is no longer proper to consider California as especially a mining State. Many of the mining villages and camps along under the mountains have been wholly deserted; nearly all are decreasing in population — it is very sad and very odd to see so new a country so soon old and decaying; and the agriculture and commerce and manufactures of the State are each, even now, in advance of the mining interest in wealth and productiveness. The mining counties have fallen off twenty-five per cent in population since 1860, while that of the agricultural counties has doubled, and that of San Francisco trebled in the same time. The agricultural products of 1868 footed up sixty millions of dollars, against twenty-six millions in metals. There are thirty million grape-vines growing in the State; and the wine manufactured in 1866 amounted to from three to four millions of gallons, and in 1868 to eight millions. The wine was at first crude and coarse, but, as the virulent richness of the soil is tempered by use, and greater care and science are used in the manufacture, its quality rapidly improves. Finer kinds of the grape than the old Mission are coming rapidly into cultivation, and will still more surely improve the quality and diversify the varieties of the wine. The wheat crop of California in 1868 was fifteen millions of bushels; the barley, eight millions, — this grain being fed freely to horses on the Pacific coast; the wool, fifteen millions of pounds; the butter, five millions, and the cheese, three millions, and still much butter and cheese are imported from the East. The exports of domestic produce, aside from metals, amounted to seventeen millions in 1868; the chief item being wheat, of

CALIFORNIA AT LARGE. 89

which no other State in the Union raised so large a surplus in that year, and, with a contribution of four million bushels of surplus from Oregon, California is holding over for higher prices, or the contingency of a bad year, probably close on to a two years' supply, for her own wants.

With such suddenly developed, yet securely held wealth as these few facts illustrate, the future of California looms before the visitor with proportions that astound and awe. Her nature is as boundless in its fecundity and variety as it is strange and startling in its forms. While Switzerland has only four mountains that reach as high as thirteen thousand feet, California has one or two hundred, and one, Mount Whitney, that soars to fifteen thousand feet, and is the highest peak of the Republic. She has a waterfall fifteen times as high as Niagara. All climates are her own; any variety which her long stretch north and south does not present, her mountains and valleys introduce. Dead volcanoes and sunken rivers abound in her mountains; the largest animal of the continent makes his covert in her chaparral; the second largest bird of the world floats over her plains for carrion; the bones of the oldest man have been dug out of her depths; the biggest nugget of gold (weighing 195 pounds and worth $ 37,400) has been found among her gold deposits; she has lakes of such rarity that a sheet of paper will sink in their waters, so voracious that they will eat up a man, boots, breeches, and all, in thirty days, so endowed in their fountains that they will supply the world's apothecaries with borax, sulphur, and soda; she has mud volcanoes and the Yosemite Valley; she grows beets of 120 pounds, cabbages of 75, onions of 4, turnips of 26, and watermelons of 80 pounds, and has a grape-vine 15 inches thick, and bearing 6,500 pounds in one season. Her men are the most enterprising and audacious; her women the most self-reliant and the most richly dressed; and her children the stoutest, sturdiest, and the sauciest of any in all the known world! Let us worship and move on!

VIII.

THE SANDWICH ISLANDS.

TO us of the East the Sandwich Islands are a remote foreign kingdom, where our whalers refit, and to the conversion of whose heathen we dedicated all the sanctified pennies of our childhood. But here in California they are counted as neighbors, dependencies, ay, surely and soon possessions of the American Republic. We have converted their heathen; we have possessed their sugar-plantations; we furnish the brains that carry on their government, and the diseases that are destroying their natives; we want the profit on their sugars and their tropical fruits and vegetables; why should we not seize and annex the islands themselves? At any rate, the familiarity with which the Eastern visitor finds "the Islands" spoken of in California, the accounts he receives of their strange scenery, their wonderful volcanoes, their delightful climate, — all will strongly invite him to make them a visit. Indeed, though his portfolio may contain choicest specimens of coloring and of contour, — new harmonies of tint, new measures of grandeur, fresh surprises of form, — gathered in sojournings among the mountains and parks of Colorada, or in the deep canyons of the Sierra, yet he must not close it feeling that he has exhausted the revelations that this Western World has to make to him, until he has added a few sketches at least of the yet more unique scenery of the Hawaiian Islands. So, if time permits, let us see the utmost possibilities and varieties of the Republic, and devote to these at least a couple of months.

This little group of breezy, sunny islands, standing like an outpost of the great army of islands, little and big, that guard the eastern coast of Asia, yet offering itself as a kind of neutral ground on which the Eastern and Western Worlds have met and joined hands, lies about two thousand miles southwest of San Francisco, and is brought into close communication with it by means of a semi-monthly steamer. A voyage of ten days, — days of uninterrupted sunshine and serenity on this most smiling of seas, — and the passenger will find himself rounding the bold, bare headland of Diamond Point, which stands guard over the little bay and city of Honolulu. The first view of this miniature capital of a petty kingdom can hardly fail to disappoint us; it is but a village of unpretending wooden houses, clustered for the most part around the bay, and stretching out, here and there, a long arm up into the hills toward which it slopes. But one has not come so many thousand miles from home to see a counterpart of Boston or New York, and the first walk on shore will offer a suggestion at least of the pleasure that awaits him in the thousand novel shapes and aspects of a changed hemisphere. After two or three weeks here, spent in early morning or evening gallops into the wonderful valleys of the range of hills that cut the island in two, varied with climbs to the different summits, from which, on each side of you, the little island seems to roll away and leap and tumble in great billows of green into the sea; and with the day rounded in on cool and fragrant verandas, among these intelligent, hospitable people, with whom kindness to the stranger is the first of duties,— the visitor will find it hard to believe that the other islands can promise greater attractions.

The first expedition usually made is to the active volcano Kilauea, situated on the Island of Hawaii, the easternmost of the group. For this the indispensable articles by way of outfit are, first, a waterproof (in case of a lady, a bloomer dress of heavy woollen material) and a saddle, as all the journeying must be made on horseback; to these may be added whatever articles of comfort or convenience the individual taste may suggest; but it is desirable that all should not exceed the capacity of a pair of saddle-bags. To sail direct to Hilo, which is the most common course, instead of landing on the other side of the island at Kawaihae, and making a partial circuit of the island, is to rob one's self of a rich and rare experience of pleasure. It is a journey of three or four days, and attended with some fatigue and discomfort, but to the enthusiastic sight-seer the annoyances will prove far more than overpaid by the pleasures. After a day of monotonous scenery, the road winds round the base of Mauna Kea, and comes out close to the sea; and then begins the romantic part of it, through a succession of precipices, — or great cracks, they might be called, — from one hundred to five hundred feet deep, and so steep that General Putnam's feat of riding down stairs seemed nothing to the perils of such a descent. But these palis, as the natives call them, are as beautiful as they are appalling; their steep sides are covered with every shade of green, from the silver-leaved kukui to the dark purple fronds of pulu fern, — masses and tangles of vines and trees, and at the bottom of each a roaring, tumbling brook, or narrow arm of the sea. On this side of the island, also, lie the rich sugar-plantations under whose hospitable roofs the traveller must look to find his shelter and his victual.

But Hilo will not suffer him to pass her by without stopping to pay a tribute of admiration to her beautiful bay and cultivated and generous inhabitants, giving him at the same time the opportunity to take breath before the last and longest day of his journey. Kilauea lies four thousand feet high on the side of the lofty Mauna Loa, and a gradual ascent of thirty miles lands you suddenly on the edge of its enormous, yawning chasm. So vast is it that it is impossible to get any idea of its gigantic proportions till you have climbed down its almost perpendicular walls, and traversed its ten-mile circuit. The condition of its activity varies greatly at different times; sometimes a chain of fiery lakes, connected by subterraneous channels, hems in the molten mass; sometimes it overleaps its barriers, and pours out rivers of fire over the floor of the crater. No words can depict the awful fascination of those fiery caldrons, boiling and hissing and roaring, and tossing up fountains of liquid flame. The most effective time to see them is at evening. Then the whole sky is lighted up with the reflection of the fire, and the surrounding darkness serves to heighten the effect of the glowing, seething mass.

In striking contrast with Kilauea stands the stupendous extinct volcano of Haleakala, almost the greater wonder of the two. It occupies the eastern half of the Island of Maui, and is a cone of ten thousand feet high. Its crater is three times the size of Kilauea, — that is, thirty miles in circumference, — and more than a thousand feet deep. Parties who visit this are accustomed to take their camping equipage, and to pass a night on the top of the mountain, not only because the excursion would be too fatiguing for a single day, but also because, through the day the crater is filled with light clouds and mist, which only depart with the setting sun. No scene could possibly combine more elements of the grand and the beautiful than this does; the soft flocculent masses of clouds silently rolling in and out of these Tartarean depths, through the great gap in the mountain-wall, toward the sea, occasionally breaking to reveal the frightful darkness beneath; then, as the sun sinks, it touches the whole cloud-landscape with a rose-gray glow; long lines of trade-wind cloudlets, like fleets of phantom ships, go scudding over the sea; the three lofty summits of Hawaii, and the lesser heights of the islands surrounding Maui, repeat the sunset tints, and the whole seems like a scene of enchantment. Maui also can boast of a valley that deserves to be mentioned by the side of the Yosemite, though different enough in outline and in coloring to forbid rivalry; and these, together with the most picturesque mountain group of all the islands, the richest sugar-plantations, and the most generous and free-handed proprietors, make for Maui the greenest spot in the memory of every traveller.

It is impossible, in the limits of such a brief sketch as this, to do more than roughly outline the chief points of interest of these far-off islands. The climate, too, lends its subtle attraction, being just that delicious blending of heat and coolness that leaves one puzzled to know whether he is only comfortably warm or refreshingly cool. One who has two or three months of leisure cannot better bestow it than in going to see all this for himself; and he will obtain from the warm-hearted islanders every possible help and suggestion he may need to make his journey easy and profitable, with only one drawback, and that is, that at every place he may stop, with the exception of Honolulu, he must accept the freely-offered hospitality of the foreign residents, nor dare to make any return, except in friendship's coin.

IX.

OREGON. — PUGET'S SOUND. — THE COLUMBIA RIVER.

THE Islands, however, involve, with the rest, a full five or six months, and cannot be put into the two or three months' plan with which we left home. But Oregon, the Columbia River, and Idaho can ; and if you please we will go home that way. It will take but two weeks longer than the straight railroad line back, and even the most superficial circuit of our New West will be incomplete without it. Good ocean steamers will carry us around to Portland, Oregon, from San Francisco within two days; but if the roads are tolerable and the stage service what it should be, we shall prefer to go overland. The cars take us up the grand valley of the Sacramento through Marysville to Oroville, and leave about five hundred miles for the stage. We ride then through broad, alluvial meadows, golden brown with wheat, enlivened by a frequent old oak grove; past Chico, where, if possible, we should linger to see General Bidwell, and his twenty-thousand-acre farm, with gardens and orchards to correspond; past Red Bluffs, the head of navigation on the Sacramento River, where the widow and daughters of old John Brown live in quiet village honor and usefulness, nursing the sick, teaching the young; into narrowing valleys, the Coast Range and the Sierras meeting and embracing each other; over pleasant hills with occasional plantations of apple, pear, and grape, growing here most luxuriantly; along under the grand shadows of Mount Shasta, monarch of the Northern Sierras, and the Mont Blanc of California; over higher hills and into the cross valleys of Northern California and Southern Oregon, — the Trinity, Klamath, Rogue, and Umpqua Rivers coursing wildly to the sea, — many a gem of oak grove on the way, the green misletoe and the gray moss pendent from the branches, and the gay madrona-tree lighting up the scene; many a broad intervale of grass and grain welcoming flocks or reapers; through and in sight of forests of pines, cedars, spruces, balsams, birches, and ash, greener and more diversified than those of California, and grander in individual size and collective extent than those of the Alleghanies or the White Hills, — stopping in the Umpqua valley to have an hour's chat on the philosophy and practice of politics with Jesse Applegate, a wise old pioneer of Oregon, — finding everywhere beauty, novelty, and exhilaration in nature; and come out at last into the garden of Oregon, the Willamette valley. Never elsewhere have our eyes looked upon a scene of picturesque rural beauty like that spread before us, as the stage comes out of the hills and woods, and we overlook the broad meadows, with their wide, open groves, rising and falling in softly undulating lines, and the hills standing far apart to frame the picture. The parks of Old England, the valleys of New England, the prairies of Illinois, the mountains of Colorado and California, all seem to have contributed their special elements, their choicest treasures, to make up this scene. Through this valley of the Willamette (or Wallomet, as some of the Oregonians insist on spelling the name), one hundred and twenty-five miles long and fifty miles wide, the railroad or the steamboat may quicken our speed; but we shall wish to linger over its wealth of beauty and wealth of agriculture. Prosperous villages lie along the river, and sixty thousand people already live upon the soil. Wheat, corn, and fruit are the chief products; and there is no stint in the return.

Portland lies on the Willamette, just before it enters the Columbia, has from eight to nine thousand inhabitants, who pay almost a New England respect to the Sabbath, and dreams sometimes that it is a rival to San Francisco. It would be well if, now we are here, we could run across Washington

Territory, — a two days' ride through thicker forests of larger trees even than any we have before seen, always excepting the grand mammoth groves of California, — and visit that northern wealth of water, Puget's Sound. Steamboats carry us through it to Victoria, on Vancouver's Island, and back, and the ride is a revelation of new beauties and new wealth. Magnificent forests line its shores; the largest ships can move close to its banks; there is lumber here for all nations and all time; snow-covered mountains, grand in form, smiling in visage, rise on the right and left; and we come back penetrated with a new wonder at the far-reaching bounty of our Northwest, and a trifle impatient that the British drum-beat is even temporarily sounded over a portion of such waters, over an acre of such excellent forests for ship-timber and profitable lumber generally. A week's time would suffice to make this excursion from Portland to Victoria and back, and most recompensing investment would it prove.

But we promised to return homeward by the

Columbia River. Elegant steamers convey us into and up its mile-and-a-half broad sea-sweep. Soon we pass Fort Vancouver, where Grant, Hooker, and McClellan all served apprenticeship, and Grant distinguished himself by raising a crop of potatoes; and it was while here, too, that our new President left the army, to come back in the hour of national distress, — rescued himself, rescuing us. Mount Hood appears next upon the scene, the pride of Oregon, and fit rival to California's Shasta, — indeed, a grand pyramid of snow in the distance; but soon now we enter the exciting theatre of conflict between river and rock, that distinguishes the Columbia River above all other known rivers, and endows it with a beauty and a grandeur that the Rhine, the Hudson, and the Northern Mississippi can hardly unitedly claim. Two short railroads of five and fourteen miles convey passengers and freight around rapids and rocks in the river, where boats cannot pass, to other boats of equal excellence above.

X.

IDAHO.— SHOSHONE FALLS.

EAST of the mountains the close, rich forests disappear, the hills are bare and brown as in Nevada, and the boat-ride grows monotonous. At Umatilla or Walla-Walla, some three hundred miles above Portland, we come to the present head of navigation, and take stages for a ride of five hundred miles over the Blue Mountains, through the Grande Ronde valley, along the valley of the Snake River, where steamboats can and may soon help us over another one hundred and fifty miles of the way, into and through Idaho, and on to Salt Lake and the railroad again. That portion of this ride over the Blue Mountains and through the Grande Ronde Valley is most satisfactory for scenery. The ascent and descent of the mountains are easy, the roads hard and smooth, and the views, near and remote, very grand and inspiring. Gorges and parks, forests and meadows alternate with fine panoramic effect; and a bath in the warm sulphur springs by the roadside will relieve the weariness of the body. Through Idaho, whose gold-mines seem to hesitate in their productiveness, and whose towns are either fading or at a standstill, and along the Upper Snake, the country bears a dull, barren uniformity, and high volcanic table-lands begin to appear and absorb the landscape.

Here, within from one hundred to one hundred and thirty miles of the north end of Salt Lake, are to be found several peculiar and grand freaks of Nature, which the traveller should leave the stage for a day or two to observe. The first, coming east, is the canyon of the Malade River, a branch of the Snake on the north; for miles it flows through a narrow gorge of solid lava rock, in some places fifty feet deep, and yet only eight or ten feet across, the confined waters coursing rapidly and angrily along below. Next, at Snake River

Ferry, the waters of its Lost River Branch, having sunk beneath the ground a long distance back, emerge to light again just at the point of junction, and pour over rocks one hundred and fifty feet high into the main stream. Ten or fifteen miles from this point, though only seven miles from the stage-road at another place, are the Shoshone Falls in the Snake River itself. They rank next to Niagara in the list of the world's waterfalls, and by some visitors are held to be entitled to the first rank in majesty of movement and grandeur of surrounding feature. All about is volcanic rock, — wide lava fields give an awful silence for this grand voice of Nature to speak in. The river, two hundred yards wide, deep and swift, has worn itself a channel one hundred feet down into the rock; then, as if in preparation for the grand leap, it indulges in a series of cascades of from thirty to sixty feet in height, and, now gathering into an unbroken body, it swoops down, in a grand horseshoe shape, twelve hundred feet across, a two hundred and ten feet fall, into the bottomless pit below. The river is not so wide as Niagara, nor the volume of water so great, but the fall is higher, and quite as beautiful. It is difficult to get near to the falls, because of the high, rough, and perpendicular walls of rock that guard the stream; but they can be reached with hard climbing both above and below. A perpendicular pillar of rock rises one hundred feet in the midst of the rapids above; islands halt in the stream just over the cataract; and two huge rocky columns stand on each side of the falls, as if to sentinel the scene, and guard it from sacrilegious hands. Either by a day's detour in the trip from the Columbia River to Salt Lake, as we have suggested, or by a special journey of three or four days from the railroad at the latter point, these distinctive and distinguished marvels of nature will soon be freely visited by Pacific Railroad travellers, and the details of their sublimity more thoroughly catalogued by pen and photograph for the general public.

XI.

MONTANA AND HOME.

NOW again at Salt Lake, — time, money, and disposition holding out, and the season favorable, — there will, indeed, be great temptation to round our travel with the stage ride through Montana to Fort Benton on the Upper Missouri, and follow down that river in one of its steamboats to Omaha again. It is about three hundred miles by stage to Virginia City, Montana, four hundred and twenty-five to Helena, and near six hundred to Fort Benton, and the fare through one hundred and forty dollars. The roads are excellent, the stage service the best on the continent, and the scenery across the high, open plains, along the fertile valleys, and through the favorable passes in the upper Rocky Mountain ranges, fresh, picturesque, and every way inviting. Colorado is scarcely more favorable for farming and stock-growing purposes than Montana. The ride is among the head-waters of the Missouri River, and grand mountains follow as guides and guards, and yet not to obstruct, along the entire pathway. In Montana, too, we can see mining in all its phases, more readily than perhaps anywhere else, — by paning, "long toms," sluicing, hydraulics, and quartz-mills; each and all are in operation there now and near together. The boat ride down the Missouri will be long, slow, and tedious; the stream is muddy, the banks for the most part high, barren, and uninviting; the time will perhaps be ten days or two weeks; but the experience will prove very instructive, and the journey will afford opportunity for reaping and digesting all the summer harvest of the senses.

Or, postponing Montana for a more convenient season, and indulging our unsatisfied curiosity in another peep over Brigham Young's garden and harem wall, and our weary bodies in another bath in the warm pools of fresh sulphur water in the suburbs of Salt Lake City, we close our Pacific Railroad excursion by a two days' ride in the cars, back over the mountains and across the plains to Omaha, which places us again on the threshold of the East and of Home.

Over all this country, through which we have so hastily travelled, the careful hand of science has yet but little passed. Professor Whitney has done much to map the past and present of California, and inventory its varied resources; if sustained by the State, he will complete a work that will be of incalculable benefit to its people, and a great gift to the scientific knowledge of the world. Several young graduates of his survey, with aid from the general government, are fast completing a thorough scientific examination and report of a belt across the continent, along the fortieth parallel, or the line of the Pacific Railroad. This will prove of great interest and value. Professor Powell, an enthusiast in geology and natural history from Illinois, spent last summer, with a party of assistants, in a scientific exploration of the parks and mountains of Colorado, and, after wintering in the wilds of Western Colorado, he proposes this season to extend his observations into the almost unknown land of Southwestern Colorado and Northeastern Arizona, and perhaps test the safety of the passage of the great canyon of the Colorado of the West. Here lies, as yet, the grand geographical secret of our Western empire. For three hundred miles this river, which drains the western slopes of the Rocky Mountains for several hundred miles, is confined within perpendicular rock walls, averaging three thousand feet in height, down which there is no safe descent, up which there is no climbing, between which the stream runs furiously. One man is reported to have gone through it, and come out alive; to explore it, and report upon it, is the dangerous yet fascinating undertaking of Professor Powell. For the rest, our scientific knowledge of the mountains and plains and deserts of our far West depends upon the reports of government engineers, and the railroad surveys, — valuable, indeed, but incomplete, and provoking rather than allaying the curiosity of the scholar.

The Indians are not likely to interfere with Pacific Railroad travel. The fears of travellers may be spared on that account. Neither among the parks and mountains of Colorado, nor in the valleys of California and Oregon, nor in the Sierra Nevada mountains, shall we be likely to meet them, save as humble, peaceful supplicants for food and tobacco. They may appear on the routes through Idaho and Montana. But greater danger is to be apprehended from "the road agents," or highway robbers. In Nevada and California, and in Idaho, they have occasionally introduced the Mexican banditti style of operating on travellers; rarely killing their victims, and only making sure to get all their money and watches, and whatever treasure the express messenger on the stage may have in hand. This Western country is destined, probably, to go through an era of that sort of crime. The vicious and vagrant populations that followed the progress of the railroad in its building, and have been set loose by its completion, and the similar elements turned adrift by the failure of mining enterprises, both furnish the needy and desperate characters for the business. Not unlikely they may grow bold enough to stop and "go through" a railroad train. Short and sharp should be the dealing with this class of marauders, when they begin their career, and then it will speedily close. But the chance of being victims of their interference with our journeyings is not great enough to excuse any of us in staying at home, when such inviting pleasures and such wide-reaching experiences as the Pacific Railroad, open, offers to us all, lay along, around, and beyond its track.

These are but scant outlines of the new and larger half of our Republic. We have given lines where only pages could properly picture a scene, describe an experience, or develop a capacity.

Arizona, New Mexico, and Lower California — three territories as remarkable, perhaps, in natural wonders and resources as any in our New West — have hardly been touched upon; but only speculators or adventurers will be readily tempted into their difficulties and dangers now; and we fear the early travellers by the new pathway of iron will be appalled by the variety of entertainment to which we here invite them. But if they start with the protest that we have promised too much, they will return with the confession that the half was not told them.

Whatever we go out to see, whatever pleasures we enjoy, whatever disappointments suffer, this, at least, will be our gain, — a new conception of the magnitude, the variety and the wealth, in nature and resource, in realization and in promise, of the American Republic, — a new idea of what it is to be an American citizen. He is past appeal and beyond inspiration who is not broadened, deepened, greatened, every way, by such experience of the extent, capacity, and opportunity of this Nation, and who does not henceforth perform his duties as its citizen with increased fidelity and a more sacred awe of his trust.

APPENDIX.

OUTLINE FOR A TWO MONTHS' JOURNEY TO THE PACIFIC STATES BY THE PACIFIC RAILROAD.

	Days.
From Omaha to Cheyenne and Denver	2
Excursions in Colorado	9
To Salt Lake City	2
Stay in Salt Lake City	2
To Virginia City, and there	2
To San Francisco, with two days to stop on the way	3
In and about San Francisco	7
Yosemite Valley and Big Trees	10
Overland to Oregon	6
From Portland to Victoria, through Washington Territory and Puget's Sound, and back	7
From Portland to Salt Lake by Columbia River, Idaho, and Shoshone Falls	8
From Salt Lake to Omaha	2
Total	60

This is obviously a short allowance for so comprehensive a journey; but every traveller can enlarge it to suit his comfort and convenience. He cannot advantageously cut down Colorado, San Francisco and its neighborhoods, or the Yosemite, but may well add a week to each. Another month would allow the traveller to return through Montana and down the Upper Missouri, besides scattering an extra week along through the previous portions of his journey. Two months more still — or from June 1 to November 1 — would include, with all the above, a liberal excursion to the Sandwich Islands. And the weather in all these five months would be favorable for every part of the grand trip; only in the Islands would waterproofs and umbrellas be needed. For the two months' journey we would recommend July and August; for the three, July, August, and September. California is in its summer glory in April and May; but that is too early for its mountains or the Yosemite; and the parks and mountains of Colorado, though passable in June, are much more accessible in July and August.

Table of Railroad Distances between the Atlantic and Pacific Oceans.

	Miles.
New York to Chicago	963
Boston to Chicago	1,019
Chicago to Omaha	490

Pacific Railroad.

	Miles.	
Omaha to Grand Island	154	154
Grand Island to North Platte	137	291
North Platte to Sidney	123	414
Sidney to Cheyenne	102	516
[Branch road to Denver, 110 miles.]		
Cheyenne to Laramie	56	572
Laramie to Bryan	286	858
Bryan to Church Buttes	27	885
Church Buttes to Bridger	27	912
Bridger to Echo City	74	986
Echo City to Ogden	44	1,030
[Branch road to Salt Lake City, 40 miles, and point of union of the Central Pacific and Union Pacific roads.]		
Ogden to Corinne, Bear River	24	1,054
Corinne to Promontory City	29	1,083
[Stage lines for Idaho and Montana.]		
Promontory to Monument Point	27	1,110

APPENDIX.

Monument Point to Humboldt Wells	142	1,252
Humboldt Wells to Elks	56	1,308
[Stage line to White Pine.]		
Elks to Carlin	23	1,331
Carlin to Argenta	49	1,380
[Stage line to Austin.]		
Argenta to Humboldt	141	1,521
Humboldt to Wadsworth	68	1,589
Wadsworth to Reno	34	1,623
[Branch to Virginia City, 17 miles.]		
Reno to Truckee	35	1,658
Truckee to summit of Sierra Nevadas	14	1,672
Summit to Dutch Flat	39	1,711
Dutch Flat to Colfax	12	1,723
Colfax to Sacramento	55	1,778
Sacramento to Stockton	45	1,823
Stockton to San Francisco	79	1,902
Chicago to San Francisco		2,392
New York to San Francisco		3,355
Boston to San Francisco		3,411

THE END.

Printed by Welch, Bigelow, and Company.

OUR NEW WAY ROUND THE WORLD;

OR,

WHERE TO GO AND WHAT TO SEE.

BY

CHARLES CARLETON COFFIN.

One volume. 540 pages. Printed from new, large-sized, clear type, containing several full-page Maps, showing steamship lines and routes of travel, and profusely illustrated with more than 100 engravings, reproduced from photographs and original sketches.

Crown octavo. Morocco Cloth. Price, $3.00.

The author of this volume is the well-known correspondent "CARLETON" of the *Boston Journal*, whose letters during the war were admired wherever read, for their plain, clear, concise narrative. He left the United States in July, 1866, and has recently returned, having made the tour of the world.

It is believed that no letters have ever been given to the American public which have been so universally accepted and praised as those written by Mr. Coffin during the last eight years.

Mr. Coffin's present volume is one of unusual importance, embodying an account of his recent travels round the globe. In view of the recent completion of the Pacific Railroad, which has made Canton and Shanghae our near neighbors, it possesses peculiar interest, not only to the general reader, but to every one interested in the development of the commerce of the country, inasmuch as it gives in detail just the kind of information which the people of the United States require in relation to China, Japan, and India. It is full of information upon the manners and customs of the people of those countries, their present condition, their future prospects, and their social life; also upon the great changes now taking place in those vast empires, embracing half the population of the globe. To the traveller, "Our New Way round the World" will be an indispensable guide-book, showing him what route to take in his journey, what steamships and railway connections are to be made, what points are worthy of his attention, and furnishing him with numerous useful hints touching the expenses by the way.

** *For sale by all booksellers, or sent, post-paid, to any address, by the Publishers,*

FIELDS, OSGOOD, & CO.,
124 Tremont Street, Boston.

FOURTH EDITION.

OLDTOWN FOLKS,

BY

HARRIET BEECHER STOWE,

AUTHOR OF "UNCLE TOM'S CABIN," "AGNES OF SORRENTO," ETC.

One vol. 12mo. 616 pages. Price, $2.00.

"It is the first novel which Mrs. Stowe has written since 1862, and is one of the best she ever wrote, so far as regards the power of its character-drawing, the richness of experience developed, the delicate humor and genuine pathos of its descriptions, and its all-pervading tenderness, catholicity of spirit and comprehension of the most various types of character.

"It is in the autobiographic form, and the few incidents of a plot remarkably simple and straightforward are skilfully made to serve as connecting links to a series of portraits of typical New England characters, as developed in all of their original and peculiar features during the generation which came to maturity at the time of the Revolution, and during the next succeeding years." — *New York Evening Mail.*

"It exhibits actual New England life, in the ante-railway times, and while the element of pathos is not deficient, the volume abounds in racy humor. Above all, it is rich in delineations of character, — not mere sketches, put here and there upon the canvas, in isolated situations, as if they had very little connection with the action of the story, but moving through it like things of life, and so peopling the various scenes that the most insignificant among them would be missed. This is very high commendation, but Mrs. Stowe fully merits it. Her various personages are not portraits, but men, women, and children, with whom we became thoroughly acquainted as we went through the story. There is not a thing done nor a word said in this story that one can honestly affirm is not exactly in accordance with human nature, in such or such circumstances of action and utterance. Even Sam, who talks a great deal, in a very peculiar *patois*, does not speak too much. Finally, with regret for being unable, from limited space, to give some extracts, we have to pronounce 'Oldtown Folks' a charming and very original story." — *Philadelphia Press.*

** *For sale by all Booksellers. Sent, post-paid, on receipt of price, by the Publishers,*

FIELDS, OSGOOD, & CO.,
124 Tremont Street, Boston.

TWENTY-THIRD EDITION.

THE GATES AJAR.

BY

E. STUART PHELPS.

One vol. 16mo.　　.　　.　　Price, $1.50.

This powerful and original story has excited general interest, both by the novel views presented concerning the future life, and by the fascinating style in which the story is told.

"The Gates Ajar is the title of a small but significant volume. On a slender thread of incident, — the story of a great sorrow and of its gradual consolation, told in the form of a journal, — a theory of life in heaven is set forth, and the common notions entertained of it by Christians are severely criticised. . . . . The whole volume is full of life. It is a work of genius." — *Examiner and Chronicle (New York).*

"Of all the books which we ever read, calculated to shed light upon the utter darkness of sudden sorrow, and to bring peace to the bereaved and solitary, we give — in many important respects — the preference to 'The Gates Ajar.'" — *Congregationalist (Boston).*

"Such an appeal to what is deepest, tenderest, and holiest in the human heart has been rarely made. Only a woman who has known sorrow and been sanctified by it could have conceived such a book as this; only a woman of the rarest mental gifts, and of eminent symmetry and wholeness of being, could have wrought out the conception as it is embodied in this volume." — *Morning Star.*

⁎⁎* For sale by all Booksellers. Sent, post-paid, on receipt of price, by the Publishers,

FIELDS, OSGOOD, & CO.,
124 Tremont Street, Boston.

EIGHTH EDITION.

MURRAY'S
ADVENTURES in the ADIRONDACKS.

One vol. 16mo. 8 full-page Illustrations.
Price, $1.50.

"This book is a guide to the best hunting and fishing region of America. It is more; for its descriptions are charming, and the pure gold of enchantment is thrown over them, so that the book is bewitching to a novice in the sportsman's art. It is mirthful, for we laughed until our sides ached over some of the sketches. 'The Ball,' and the description of 'Southwick's dancing,' we have hardly recovered from yet. 'Jack-shooting in a Foggy Night' made our very ribs sore. Some of the sketches are grand masterpieces of fine writing, and the whole work superior. We predict for it an immense sale and a multitude of enthusiastic friends." — *Providence Press.*

"His 'Adventures in the Wilderness' constitute a capital guide to those who desire to enjoy the free air of heaven and free life by field and flood. There is a great deal of subdued humor and quiet fun in the pages before us; that Jack-shooting adventure is related with great spirit; 'Running the Rapids' kept us almost breathless while we read; 'Phantom Falls' is a weird narrative: and, as a quiet and thoughtful production, let us commend 'Sabbath in the Woods' to readers of all moods of mind." — *Philadelphia Press.*

*** *For sale by all Booksellers. Sent, post-paid, on receipt of price, by the Publishers,*

FIELDS, OSGOOD, & CO.,
124 Tremont Street, Boston.

www.ingramcontent.com/pod-product-compliance
Lightning Source LLC
Chambersburg PA
CBHW031346160426
43196CB00007B/749